Dec. 2022
Dear Troy & John —
For Some fun memories —
Merry Christmas! Love, Gail

THEN...
SAN FERNANDO VALLEY
& Now

SAN FERNANDO

THEN...

VALLEY

& Now

GIBBS SMITH

Gibbs Smith, Publisher
Salt Lake City

First Edition

07 06 05 04 03   5 4 3 2 1

Text © 2003 Gibbs Smith Publisher

Photo captions written by Kurt Wahlner

Published by
Gibbs Smith, Publisher
P.O. Box 667
Layton, Utah 84041

Orders: (1-800) 748-5439
www.gibbs-smith.com

Edited by Suzanne Gibbs Taylor
Designed and produced by Kurt Wahlner
Printed and bound in Hong Kong

Library of Congress Cataloging-in-Publication Data

Klein, Jake.
   Then & now : San Fernando Valley / Jake Klein.— 1st ed.
      p. cm.
   ISBN 1-58685-229-9
   1. San Fernando Valley (Calif.)—History—Pictorial works.
2. San
 Fernando Valley (Calif.)—History. 3. Historic
buildings—California—San Fernando Valley. 4. Historic
sites—California—San Fernando Valley. I. Title: Then and
now. II.
 Title: San Fernando Valley. III. Title.
 F868.L8K58 2003
 979.4'93—dc21
                                              2003005239

Photo Credits

Then:

Courtesy of the Security Pacific Collection/Los Angeles Public Library, 10, 12, 16, 26, 28, 30, 34, 36, 40, 48, 54, 62

Courtesy of the Security Pacific Collection/Los Angeles Public Library/Photo by Luckhaus Studio, 58

Courtesy of the Hollywood Citizen News/Valley Times Collection/ Los Angeles Public Library, Front flap, 14, 42, 50, 56, 68, 72, 74, 84, 88

Courtesy of the Hollywood Citizen News/Valley Times Collection/ Los Angeles Public Library/Photos by George Brich, 32, 52, Back Cover (left inset)

Courtesy of the Hollywood Citizen News/Valley Times Collection/ Los Angeles Public Library/Photo by Jeff Goldwater, Front Cover (left inset), 22

Courtesy of the Hollywood Citizen News/Valley Times Collection/ Los Angeles Public Library/Photo by Jon Woods, 38

Courtesy of the Herald Examiner Collection/Los Angeles Public Library, 70, 76 (inset), 80, 82, Back Cover

Courtesy of Jake Klein, 2-3, 8, 18, 20, 24, 44, 46, 60, 64, 66, 78, 86

Now:

All *Now* photos © by Larry Bleidner, except the following:

Photos © by Jake Klein, 61, 65, and 67;
photo © by Kurt Wahlner, 3 (inset);
photo © 2003 ABC Photography Archives, 57

Overleaf: The main drag of North Hollywood— Lankershim Boulevard from Chandler Avenue looking south toward Weddington in 1924—is contrasted with the changing of the statue of Bob's Big Boy.

Introduction

Laid out like a refulgent jeweled box guarded by the rolling San Gabriels on three sides, the San Fernando Valley is a green carpet of urbanism during the day and a twinkling box of precious stones after sunset. Rows of yellow sodium lamps and green-glowing flourescents light oceans of asphalt and millions of perfect square plots, upon which sit the dreams of countless American families.

There it lies, looking over the shoulder of its big sister, Los Angeles—the Valley, as this huge swath of land just east of the California coast is known, is the much maligned and constantly debased stepchild of an equally maligned and debased parent city. Together, these two survivors tell an important tale.

Like so many places in the American West, this is a suburban refuge founded by freedom-seekers with the sweet taste of adventure on their tongues. The Valley is an encapsulation of America's history and spirit.

On Saturday, August 3, 1769, a band of hearty men and mules trudged over the pass that is roughly where the San Diego Freeway now passes under Mulholland Highway as it snakes into Bel Air and disappears toward the sea. Spread out below the explorers was an unfettered view from one mountain range clear across this valley to the next. Utter possibility stretched out before these god-fearing men. These were Spanish and Mexican citizens charged by an absent king to make the dusty trek up from distant San Diego in order to establish a land route to Monterey, the site of an important Spanish settlement.

Though the Valley was already home to native Chumash and Tongva peoples, the Spaniards claimed the place as their own. The New World was a sanctuary; its splendors were theirs for the taking. The group returned to the mission at San Diego with tales of this vast open plain. Maps were quickly drawn up: the place would be christened *El Valle de Los Encinos* and the river would be called the *Rio Porciuncula.* By the late 1700s, two huge portions of San Fernando Valley land were deeded to Spanish nationals living in the area: Jose Maria Verdugo and his brother Mariano. Still more land was given over to Francisco Reyes, an original member of the group that first stumbled upon the Valley. On September 8, 1797, a Franciscan priest declared that the land where Reyes had settled would become the next California mission. The San Fernando Valley as we know it was then born.

Like much of the American West, it would be almost a century until the true character of the San Fernando Valley began to truly take shape. Born of a desire for separate living, the Valley is a semi-rural place where people settled to be slightly removed from its high-urban neighbors. Los Angeles and the Valley had grown steadily after their settlement by the Spanish in the mid- to late-1700s, as its character took its shape in the form of a lazily sprawling metropolis. Tens of thousands of acres of rich and fertile soil were exploited by pioneering men and women who toiled in the vast fields growing wheat, apricots, and oranges. America was still a rural place, its cities always in close proximity to the agricultural operations that kept its citizens fed. As agriculture gave way to urbanism, the spirit of the plains was imbued permanently in the fabric of this new suburban model. The Valley was and still is a curious melange of rural urbanism.

The Valley was founded by dreamers. Like so many before them, these pioneers saw the flat, wide expanse as a promise of the American dream. These people divided and subdivided these rich lands to create an ordered place from what was wild and untamable just years before.

The Valley is a collection of cities founded on the notion that there is freedom in having space. It is a suburban metropolis that took root in the dry earth and grew into a rich forest, dense with cultural, ethnic, and socioeconomic diversity. The Valley, for all its flat, monotonous sprawl, is an integral part of the Southern California landscape, and there are few places in the world like it. From mechanical sharks to canonized Saints, from "mall hair" to missile defense, the Valley has played a key role in modern American history. This book is a celebration of the many cities that together make up one of America's greatest icons.

—*Jake Klein*

▲ Originally a dusty canyon pass between Cole (Hollywood) and the vast plain that was the San Fernando Valley, the Cahuenga Pass was home to Pacific Electric trolleys during the 1890s. The trolleys shared space with the few cars and horse-drawn stages that made the trip each day, transporting fruits and vegetables to the downtown Los Angeles area.

▲ The Cahuenga Pass is still a vital link between the San Fernando Valley and metropolitan Los Angeles. The Hollywood Freeway, developed in 1957, quickly became an overcrowded nightmare, clogged morning, noon, and night. The "Gateway to the Valley" surpasses San Francisco's Bay Bridge as the most heavily traveled highway link in California.

▲ While most of the Valley consisted of nothing but farmland, on March 15, 1915, Carl Leammle, Sr., dedicated Universal City. Ten thousand spectators, including Thomas Edison and Buffalo Bill Cody attended the three-day event. Here the administration building welcomes visitors to observe the moviemaking process.

▲ Universal City still welcomes visitors from around the world to observe the moviemaking process. "Uncle Carl's" filmmaking mecca is now a sprawling entertainment mecca, featuring the studio tour, hotels, the Universal Amphitheater, and the internationally imitated City Walk "shopping promenade."

▲ Not long after dentist David Burbank founded the city that bears his name, establishments such as the popular Luttge Brothers store, at the corner of Orange Grove and San Fernando, began popping up along the dirt-covered thoroughfares across the city. For many years, these general stores were the only forums of "community" for miles around.

▲ From a one-story brick building to a two-story one—now that's progress! San Fernando road continues to be a major thoroughfare in the Burbank area. Where the Luttge's store once stood, there now appears a similar structure housing a restaurant. Just two blocks away is the popular Burbank Media City Center.

▲ Equestrians have always gravitated to the area in Burbank just north of Griffith Park. Here in the late 1940s, a group of juvenile riders known as the Dusk Riders stand tall in the saddle for a big Saturday-morning ride. The Dusk Riders sometimes appeared in the San Fernando Fiesta Parade.

▲ A horsewoman takes a solitary workout in the early morning hours. The Los Angeles Equestrian Center is well known throughout the city for its mature bridle paths, horse-boarding facilities, and riding schools, and as a place where one can even watch a great polo match.

▲ The Los Angeles & San Fernando Valley Electric Railway Company announced its intention "to build an electric railway from Los Angeles to the city of San Fernando, a distance of 25 miles." The first Red Car wire was strung in May 1911.

▲ The first Red Car line was strung in 1911—then what happened? The Red Car system never really caught hold in the Valley before mass transit in Los Angeles converted to diesel-powered buses. Incredibly, Los Angeles's subway system reached Lankershim and Chandler in North Hollywood in 2000.

▲ North Hollywood became one of the Valley's first real towns. After initially being known as Lankershim, the name changed to North Hollywood to capitalize on the movie craze. Shown above is the corner of Lankershim and Weddington just prior to the opening of the El Portal Theatre in 1926.

▲ The historic El Portal Theatre building and the former Bank of America building serve as cornerstones of the North Hollywood Arts District. After standing vacant for many years, the earthquake-damaged El Portal has been extensively retrofitted and is now home to a lively theatrical production schedule.

▲ Believe it or not, the land used in the development of Studio City began with sheepherding. On the rolling hills just south of the stagecoach route, which later became Ventura Boulevard, the land was considered too steep for agricultural purposes, but the native live oak trees encouraged the growth of meadow grass.

▲ Despite the log-jam traffic along Ventura Boulevard, just blocks away, at the corner of Sunshine Terrace and Vantage Avenue, lies the bucolic atmosphere yearned for by busy career people. This is real "Ward and June Cleaver" territory. All of this peace and quiet comes at a price, however. Homes in these zip codes have the highest resale value in the Valley.

▲ Back in the early 1960s a group called "The Ventura Boulevard Merchants Association" decided to try to boost sales, so it created a "shopping night" to encourage shopping along the searchlight-swept street. These stores at the corner of Ventura and Vantage Avenue stayed open until 9 o'clock in the evening and paved the way for other merchants to keep their shops open late.

▲ The tempo of life has changed so radically in the last 40 years that along the once slow-paced Ventura Boulevard most businesses have to fight against bumper-to-bumper traffic through Studio City. The worst of it always seems to coagulate near the intersection of Ventura and—you guessed it—Vantage.

▲ The Valley has always been a great place to pull off to the side of the road and dream. What could these women be envisioning? This photo is only identified by the phrase "The Valley from Winnetka."

▲ The Valley is still best viewed from the lofty heights of Mulholland Drive (above Winnetka, of course).

▲ The concentrated development of the San Fernando Valley didn't really begin until after World War II. Before then, the rural atmosphere was what attracted so many people.

▲ Today the dry, flat expanse of the Valley has been transformed into a verdant urban forest, causing property values to skyrocket into the million-dollar range. The luxurious undergrowth creates a sense of privacy, essential for maintaining a truly Southern California lifestyle.

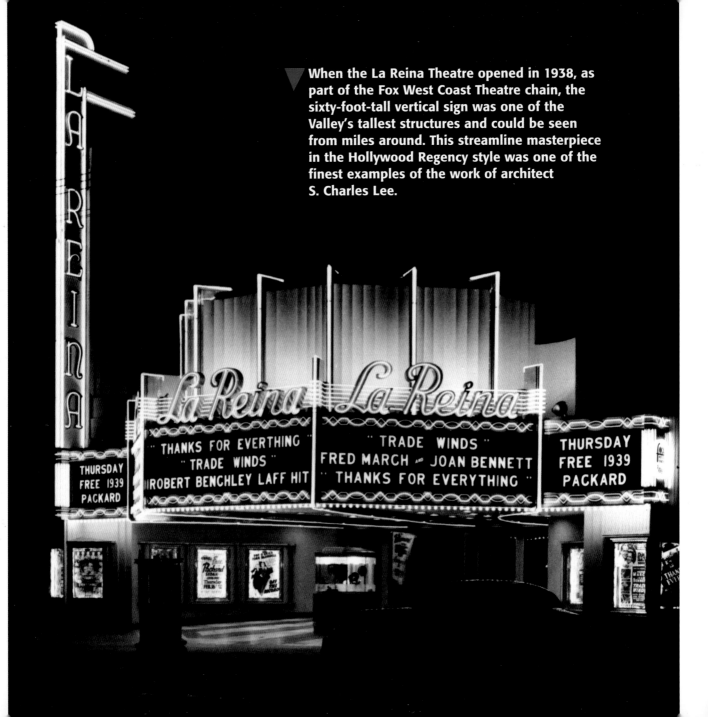

When the La Reina Theatre opened in 1938, as part of the Fox West Coast Theatre chain, the sixty-foot-tall vertical sign was one of the Valley's tallest structures and could be seen from miles around. This streamline masterpiece in the Hollywood Regency style was one of the finest examples of the work of architect S. Charles Lee.

▲ The La Reina Theatre showed its last film in 1984, but no one had the heart to tear down the beautiful façade and so it was incorporated into the superstructure of a shopping center. The vertical sign collapsed in the 1992 Northridge earthquake. After a stint as a clothing outlet and other uses, perhaps it will become a movie theater again.

▲ Movie theaters weren't the only thing going up in the valley during the years leading up to the Baby Boom. Massive housing tracts cut into the mountains south of Ventura (like this one in Sherman Oaks) would eventually call for the construction of the rest of our modern infrastructure: schools, churches, a hardware store—the works.

▲ Of course, the terracing of the Santa Monica Mountains still goes on, but the cost to develop this land is so withering that only the most affluent can afford it. No wonder the wealthy desire to have a voice in their own government. The notion of secession from Los Angeles is sure to rise again.

▲ Show us a native of the San Fernando Valley, and we will show you someone who has a soft spot in their heart for The Sportsman's Lodge in Studio City. Originally a man-made fishing tank, a restaurant was added in 1946 by David Harnig. Eventually a hotel was constructed in 1963, when this picture was snapped of a guest doing a little fishing . . .

▲ . . . but fishing isn't really allowed at The Sportsman's Lodge anymore. The place has just recently emerged after a six-million-dollar face-lift/renovation, and while the windows of the dining room still look out at this pastoral scene, the Lodge has garnered quite a reputation for the Salsa nightclub it hosts on Friday nights!

▲ Rancho Encinos in 1910. This view, looking north across the Valley toward Northridge, shows just how little vegetation there was in this flood-prone area. After the devastating floods of 1938, this area would later become known as the Sepulveda Dam Flood Control Area, surrounded by earthworks created from dirt scooped out of the Sepulveda Pass.

▲ Since the system of storm drains, concrete river beds, and flood control canals built in the 1950s and '60s has been so successful in dealing with flooding, the Sepulveda Dam Flood Control Area has been turned into a recreation center. There are places here where the Los Angeles River actually reverts back to its "pre-concrete" condition, much to the delight of the waterfowl.

▲ So, this is what it must have been like in Encino on the Fourth of July in the middle 1930s. Isolated, easygoing, and relaxed, there was a real community spirit to the place back then, exemplified by this outpouring at the Encino Store, located at Ventura and Genesta.

▲ Commerce has an entirely different feel in Encino now. The mom-and-pop stores have all been replaced with newer, fancier places. The Encino Marketplace has only been in operation for a few years, but already there are signs showing that it too will be replaced with something more up-to-date sooner or later.

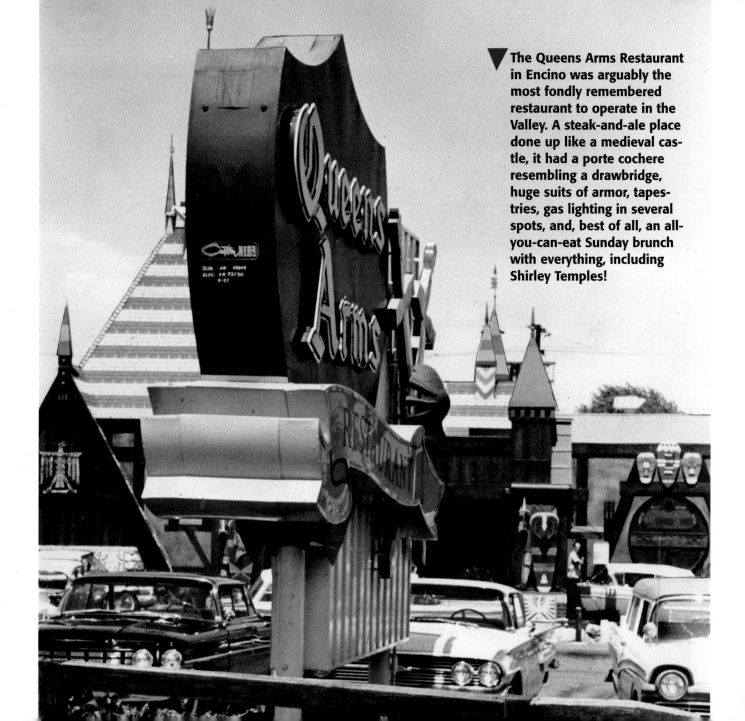

The Queens Arms Restaurant in Encino was arguably the most fondly remembered restaurant to operate in the Valley. A steak-and-ale place done up like a medieval castle, it had a porte cochere resembling a drawbridge, huge suits of armor, tapestries, gas lighting in several spots, and, best of all, an all-you-can-eat Sunday brunch with everything, including Shirley Temples!

▲ Little do the browsers at Barnes & Noble know that the store they are standing in used to house such imagi-
native enterprises. The Queens Arms shuttered in the late 1970s, but no one could stand to see it torn down,
so it stood empty for years as a reminder of an increasingly distant past. Eventually the Queens Arms,
Fletcher Jones Chevrolet and a Mobil gas station were torn down to accommodate the Encino Marketplace.

▲ The Eugene Garnier home on the grounds of Rancho Encino was built from limestone around 1869, making it the oldest structure standing in the Valley. The home features mission-type construction with walls two feet thick and outside connecting doors. The area also had an amazing artesian spring, which drew American Indians to the area for hundreds of years.

▲ Today the Garnier home is part of Los Encinos State Historic Park, a five-acre respite from the bustle, bordered by Ventura Boulevard, Moorpark Street, La Maida Street, and Balboa Boulevard. The artesian spring still flows (under a spring house), feeding a flourishing duck pond and creating a popular spot for picnics, parties, and weddings.

▲ In the well-to-do communities of Sherman Oaks, Encino, Tarzana, and Woodland Hills, the desire to add a swimming pool to one's manse was simply overwhelming. With over 24,000 of them by 1960 and with 4,000 more every year until a slowdown occurred in the 1990s, the San Fernando Valley had the highest per-capita ratio of population to swimming pools of anywhere on Earth.

▲ Heaven help the developer who does not have a swimming pool in the master plan now. The image people have in their minds when they seek housing in the Valley demands a pool, whether they are buying or renting. See the people in the picture? They are just thinking about what it would be like to live in that house. (They haven't written the down-payment check yet.)

▲ Imagine back in 1919, that a man could stand on a hill like the one above, look out over the vast tracts of land under cultivation, and say to himself: "I think I shall purchase this land. The price General Harrison Otis wants for it is fair. I think I shall call it—TARZANA!" The man? Edgar Rice Burroughs, who had just struck it rich with a novel called *Tarzan of the Apes*.

▲ And today a man will stand on these same hills, look out over the vast tracts of housing developments and feverish economic activity and ask, "Just where has the Burroughs Estate gone to anyway?" While the estate is mostly centered around the present El Cabrillo Country Club (established 1927), one can still appreciate this smog-free vista on occasion.

▲ One of the delights of following the fortunes of the San Fernando Valley is to notice the things that change—and the things that remain the same. This shot shows the intersection of Ventura Boulevard and DeSoto Avenue in Woodland Hills, where a fire hydrant had been decapitated. Everything is there: the street, the freeway overpass, and the hills of Pierce College.

▲ But where are all of these things now? There is nothing recognizable here from the other shot. What's going on here? We thought the whole point was to show what was there "then" and what is there "now." What has happened is that in the years since the "then" photo was taken, the 20900 block has slipped toward the West. It is now at Ventura and Alhama.

▲ Here is a building that really got a workout! The Reseda Community Center and Plunge in Reseda Park as it appeared sometime before opening to the public in the summer of 1937. This date makes it one of the oldest public swimming pools in the state. For "whites only" originally, it was segregated until 1964.

▲ Things picked up a great deal with the construction of Reseda High School just across the Los Angeles River in 1955. Generations of high schoolers have come to look upon the Community Center as an extension of the school itself. There are extra tennis courts, basketball courts, the pool, as well as extra space for that other well-known high-school pastime: the occasional rumble.

▲ With the end of World War II, and the filling of the Valley with burgeoning families, the Golden Age of California Education began. Reseda High School was completed in 1955 at a cost of over $5,000,000. It was the most modern and up-to-the-minute facility. Enrollment into the mid-70s was 90 percent white.

▲ Reseda High School in the 1970s utilized the practice of busing to make the student population more diverse, but now the enrollment is mostly Latino. When are they going to get a new stadium? The one they have now is puny! A new one might allow Reseda to claim some of the football glory that has always eluded it in the past.

▲ Granada Hills is represented by this shot, taken in 1961, of the busy (but orderly) intersection of Chatsworth Street and Zelzah. This is actually a transition spur from the northbound Zelzah to the eastbound Chatsworth.

▲ Everything is still pretty much the same today. The trees are taller, and the U.S. and state flags have been added to the median strip, and the heavy old Chevies have been replaced with heavy Cadillac Escalades. But this still remains a busy intersection near the post office, the Granada Village shopping center, and the Cal State Northridge campus.

▲ The Chatsworth Methodist Church was chartered at the Methodist Conference in 1888. Now all they had to do was build a church building. The building volunteers watched as the cornerstone with church papers and a Bible were placed in the ground, covered with tin, and their beautiful house of worship arose over it. It was completed in 1903.

▲ With the growth in the Valley during the 1950s reaching critical mass, the church needed more space for—you guessed it—parking, so the congregation decided to acquire land and build a new church building. The lovely old structure was declared a historical monument by the city in 1963, and was moved to the Oakwood Memorial Park by the Chatsworth Historical Society in 1965.

▲ The community of Northridge was originally ostensibly "whites only"; there was *de facto* segregation. Blacks could buy houses, but none ever did until 1961, when the Wade Rice family moved in. The first African American family in Northridge was front-page material for local newspapers and the focus of many media reports.

▲ The "beautiful symphony of brotherhood" Martin Luther King dreamed about occurs in some parts of the Valley, and the African American suburban family is a regular staple of television programming. *My Wife and Kids* is filmed in the Valley on a soundstage on the Disney Studio lot in Burbank.

▲ Viennese-born film director Josef von Sternberg came to Hollywood and directed Marlene Dietrich in a number of huge hits for Paramount, so it made sense for him to have fellow Viennese Richard Neutra design the ultimate in Hollywood digs. This streamlined steel and glass beauty was completed in 1935.

▲ There is a gated cluster of security condominiums there now. Josef von Sternberg was forced out of his Paramount contract in 1935, directed some films in England, came back to Hollywood, semi-retired, and holed up in his modern house. When he died in 1969, the house (despite the protests of architectural historians) was sold and torn asunder.

▲ This is the one they always talk about—"The Big Flood of '38." It had rained hard in the Valley before, but there was nothing there for the torrent collecting over the floodplain to destroy. But in 1938, it was different. Flash flooding and huge runoffs killed 96 people and led to a clamor for more flood-control measures.

▲ Actually, the Army Corps of Engineers had been working on flood control in the Valley since 1935, the year that the Sepulveda Dam was mandated. It wasn't finished until 1941 however, and since then, the Valley has suffered only two big rains in 1980 and 1992.

▲ The essence of the Valley. A long strip of road stretching into the distance with hills in the background, vaguely seen through the haze and smog. This is Reseda Boulevard, looking South from Devonshire Boulevard in 1929.

▲ It's pretty much the same today. Only now houses have covered the plain, stores and other businesses have lined the major roads, Corvettes and pickups have replaced the Model Ts, and many people believe that the air above the Valley has fewer pollutants now than there were in the 1960s. All the better to see the long strip of road stretching into the distance.

▲ For many people, Van Nuys has always been the cornerstone of public life in the Valley. The DMV, the hall of justice, the police department—everything seems to be here. One almost takes on a different air when one is in governmental presence. It may have affected the people in this photo loitering about the branch of the local bank in the late 1920s.

▲ Van Nuys somehow keeps rolling along. The Civic Center is host to an astounding array of government services, including a new State of California office building, which will be completed soon.

▲ Van Nuys High School was the second high school to open in the Valley. The first one was San Fernando High. Van Nuys High opened in early 1914, with its first graduating class in June 1914.

▲ The Works Progress Administration-era current administration building of Van Nuys High is seated on the old foundation of the main school building. Since opening in 1914, officials estimate that 38,000 students have graduated and walked through either of these doors with diploma in hand.

▲ In 1957, taxicab driver Earl Gervais of North Hollywood was given honors by Yellow Cab Company officials and the Burbank Police Department for his outstanding safety record during his thirty-year driving career.

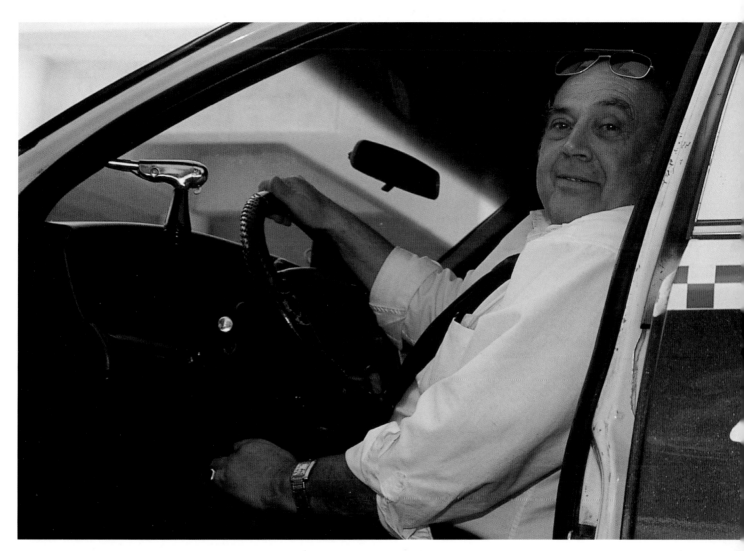

▲ This cabby is a recent immigrant from the former USSR. We don't know about his driving record, but we are sure that his cab is much safer due to the half-inch of bulletproof Lexan between him and his fares.

▲ In their loose print shirts, flared jeans, and cowboy hats, these car salesmen (perched on Grand Torinos) were waiting for customers on August 17, 1979.

▲ Today the power ties, Palm Pilots, and $300-a-pair sunglasses are all part of the ruse. Notice that the Grand Torinos have been replaced by top-of-the-line Hondas.

▲ Prior to the development of Panorama City in the 1950s (notice the first of the tract houses in the background), grazing animals were a common sight in the open fields of Van Nuys. The new subdivision homes were snatched up by the middle class as fast as they could be built.

▲ Now, fifty years later, the Valley is still a bastion of family-friendly living. And the ambience—at least in the vast outdoor mall just east of Van Nuys Boulevard—harkens back to the rich mid-1880s culture of the Latino people who once shepherded the flocks, with a blending of Old Mexico architectural details and faux-painted scenery.

There must be stability in the Valley. There must be. We nominate the Valley Municipal Building for the symbol of architectural survival. Built in 1932 and designed by architect Peter K. Schabarum, it was meant to symbolize the upward aspirations of government to the Depression-era citizenry.

Declared a Historic-Cultural Monument of the City of Los Angeles on October 18, 1978, the building still symbolizes the upward aspirations.

▲ For real stability, nothing can compare to the Mission of San Fernando. The "Rey de Espanga" was founded on September 8, 1797 by Fray Fermin Francisco De Lasuen as part of the chain of Catholic missions up and down the state. The mission of the mission: Convert the natives. The church building was completed in 1806 and stood at the center of 121,000 acres of land under its auspices.

▲ The Gabrielinos—the natives who built the mission and worked the ranch—are gone, but the mission is still here, currently supervised by Monsignor Webber, who was nice enough to stop to have his picture taken. The mission was once a lone structure on the open plain, but it is now surrounded by the close confines of the city of San Fernando and a web of freeways.

▲ This photo, taken during the 1930s, is supposedly the very first residence in Burbank. It was located at the heart of the city at San Fernando Road and Angelino. It was begun shortly after the town was founded on May 1, 1887.

▲ This photo shows the very latest residential units in Burbank. They replace many of the "dingbat" apartment buildings damaged in the 1992 Northridge earthquake.

TOW-AWAY
TEMPORARY
NO PARKING
6AM TO 6PM
EXCEPT SAT & SUN

▲ Here is the center of that bustling metropolis known as Burbank, San Fernando Road looking north from Verdugo in 1951. The chamber of commerce booster-ism of the time claimed that "man had tamed the wilderness."

▲ A view of beautiful downtown Burbank today shows a dynamic mixture of economic activity, urban renewal/blight, mountain views, and shopping centers.

▲ Some would say a major page in labor relations was turned after police armed with tear gas and water cannons fired on strikers outside the Warner Bros. Studio in Burbank. The strikers had been fired by the studio for unionizing and were protesting this action. They were eventually reinstated to their jobs.

▲ The form of social protest hasn't changed, but the objectives certainly have. These protesters, hectoring the passing cars, wish to ask their fellow human beings to not "eat Babe" for breakfast and become vegetarians.

▲ Bob's Big Boy Hamburger Restaurant in Burbank—birthplace of the double-decker burger. Friday was cruiser night, and everyone was welcome to pull up their jalopies at Big Boy for friendly drive-up service and plenty of chatter.

▲ Friday is still cruiser night, but hot rods instead of jalopies line the parking lot at Bob's. They have tried to tear down Bob's Burbank several times, but there is something about the place that makes the motorheads go psycho over the idea. Now it's a cultural landmark.

▲ All in all, the San Fernando Valley has always been what a person makes of it. The farmers who cultivated these fruit trees in the Valley must have had a great vision and desire to "make something great."

▲ And this desire, this world-renowned reputation, attracts immigrants like David Chung, selling fruit at a farmers market. It can't be easy to make a living hauling fruit to market, but the Valley's limitless horizon beckons to some and fills others with dread. There will always be fellows like Mr. Chung who will have a need to fill this desire.

▲ Now that you mention it, it *has* been a while since we have seen a blonde in a swimsuit pose on top of a ladder on Van Nuys Boulevard. Miss Van Nuys wants us to know that in 1960, when this picture was taken, Van Nuys was at the distributional center of the population of the State of California, which was 13,465,000—so educational!